Mimi May Lehmann

GETTING RID OF THE CRAP

I need a simpler life

Imprint

Bibliographic information of the German National Library: The German National Library lists this publication in the German National Bibliography; detailed bibliographic data are available on the Internet at http://dnb.dnb.de.

© 2025 Mimi May Lehmann

Produced: BoD · Books on Demand GmbH, Überseering 33,

22297 Hamburg, bod@bod.de

Published: Libri Plureos GmbH, Friedensallee 273, 22763 Hamburg

ISBN: 978-3-8192-5037-8

Table of Contents

At My Wits' End

The leaves on the trees revealed their most magnificent colors, and the mist hung over the area like a cozy blanket. My beloved October. I lay on the sofa and couldn't remotely bring myself to do anything. Just thinking about my to-do list made me want to play dead. It was breathing down my neck like a silent threat. I knew that for every minute I wasted, I would have to pay later. Without energy, I sipped my coffee and looked at the clock on our white country house shelf. It was 11:30 a.m., and the minute hand ticked on relentlessly. I knew I should have been in the kitchen long ago to prepare lunch for the children. But what should I cook? I didn't have the energy to think of a menu. Actually, I didn't have time to cook. I had to tackle my to-do list that never seemed to end. Instead, every evening, it was even longer than in the morning. No matter how hard I worked, the work just didn't get any less.

I had been self-employed, working from home for seventeen years. As a business economist, I looked after wealthy entrepreneurs and managed their business and private affairs. You could also say that I was a very well-educated private secretary. In my mid-thirties, as a mom of two small children, I studied business administration by distance learning to keep my brain exercised and myself up to date with the latest developments. In any case, I loved my clients and my work. I got to know interesting people whose elite ranks you wouldn't otherwise get an insight into. I was invited to exclusive events, and sometimes, I could even bring my family.

My clients were my mentors. They taught me a lot about the right money mindset and pragmatic business management. I was honored by their trust in me and loved working together as equals. My scope of activity varied from demanding negotiations to managing the domestic staff. But now, after all these years of constant stress, I no longer had the desire or strength to keep all those to-dos in my head.

Things got even worse when we added the Tesla rental service platform, which my husband and I had been running together for a few months. The original plan was just to rent out my Tesla – a kind of car sharing because I rarely needed the vehicle. But we were overrun with rental requests, and before we knew it, we had three Teslas of our own and eight partners renting their cars through our platform. So I basically got into the Tesla rental service like a virgin, although I never really liked this baby. No question. I loved the fancy car from California; it was a true symphony of elegance. However, as an introvert, I hated interacting and having small talk with constantly new renters.

In addition, the business collaboration with my husband increasingly put a strain on our marriage. As completely harmonized as we were in our private lives, we were just as different in business matters. He, the social butterfly, was bursting with energy and couldn't stand standing still. I, the cranky loner, preferred to work unhurried and alone. In other words: the sun shone out of his ass, and I loved the rain. While he believed that one should grow by tackling unpleasant work, I felt that everyone should use their personal potential. As an anti-team player, one of the few advantages of teamwork was distributing the tasks according to our respective disposition. The whole thing ultimately culminated in me wanting to hide when my husband came around the corner in our apartment, just because I was afraid he would come at me with even more unpleasant tasks. The last thing I needed was more work or new challenges.

I was barely able to cope with everyday life. I had been running in survival mode for months. I didn't know whether I was coming or going. I worked every day, even on Sundays, hoping to start Monday more relaxed. Of course, that never happened. As soon as I opened my notebook on Monday morning, I already had countless new emails on my screen, and each one meant even more work.

Over the years, work and private life had merged unnoticed. On the one hand, this was because I worked from home. On the other hand, I had to deal with my customers' requests within 24 hours, making it impossible to draw a clear boundary between work and private life. And so it happened that my family had no weekends, holidays, or let alone vacations.

And now it seemed like this busy life was taking its toll. There was not a single day when I couldn't manage to juggle all my obligations. I would rather have moved into a barn with no heating and an outhouse than have to manage even more.

I dragged my body into the kitchen. Through the window, I watched the people walking past our house. They all had time to do sports or go for walks with friends and still had money. What had I done wrong? When exactly did I take a wrong turn in my life's path?

I was once an ambitious businesswoman and a caring mother who navigated both worlds elegantly and effortlessly. Now, all that was left of this woman was a pitiful shadow. I was a wreck who wanted to throw myself on the floor crying just thinking about my daily tasks. Every little request pushed me to the limit. Creating a menu plan for next week – unthinkable! Making breakfast for the boys – I almost collapsed just thinking about it. Where had my joy of life gone? I was only looking forward to crawling into bed at 8 p.m.

And that, even though it was fall. My absolute favorite season! I already looked forward to it in January. To the beautiful, misty days that filled me with so much happiness and bliss that I could have wallowed in them. To the soothing calls of ravens and the divine scent of burning wood that wafted from the chimneys of the old farmhouses. I loved the evening walks through our village and across the fields with my boys just before the golden hour gave way to complete darkness. But now I just wanted to fall into a coma and only wake up when my life no longer felt so incredibly difficult and stressful.

I was at the bottom – at my wits' end. And slowly I got really angry. I was angry because I felt trapped in my own life – in the stranglehold of work and condemned to plow away non-stop. I was furious that I no longer met with relatives and friends because I didn't know when I would make up for the lost working time. Since early childhood, I was an idiosyncratic free spirit, a quiet rebel who loathed nothing more than constraints and pressure of any kind. Ironically, that's precisely where I found myself now: in the abysm of all imaginable constraints and the constant pressure to get something done. And I currently saw no way to free myself from it.

With great effort, I managed to get an uneventful lunch on the table. After the boys went back to school, I was just able to bring myself to put the dishes in the dishwasher before plopping down on the sofa again. "Heartland" was on television, a Canadian series about a family that nurses neglected horses back to health on their farm in the Rocky Mountains. An idyllic world where things were quiet and leisurely. I would have loved to move there and leave all the business crap behind me. I could have mucked out the stables with Amy and driven to Hudson with Jack to get the animal feed.

As I watched Jack and Amy, I longed more and more for a simple life – a quiet, manageable existence that gave me enough time for my children, my family, and myself. In my current life, there were simply too many to-dos, too many business obligations and problems, too many fears, and too many unfounded worries.

I knew I had to talk to my husband about it. Only together could we get back on track. I had already indicated a few times that I was no longer happy; of course, he had already noticed it himself. After all, my distressed state was obvi-ous, and I wouldn't have blamed him if the pitiful sight of me had made him want to throw himself off a bridge. Lucki-ly, we had a relationship in which honest and unvarnished communication was a given.

My biggest problem was the need to keep making money. Our family system has always been structured so that my husband and I were jointly responsible for the household, children, and income. For me, the thought of leaving my husband hanging financially was unbearable. Where would the money come from if I threw in the towel and gave up my business? I was too old to live off a sugar daddy, too poor to live off my assets, and too uptight for OnlyFans. If money didn't play a role in my life, I honestly would have preferred not to work at all. I could have devoted myself completely to the children without these constant concerns about not doing full justice to either one or the other.

I wanted a timeout to figure out what to do next and what I wanted to do from the bottom of my heart. But unfortu-nately, money still played a role, and I definitely had to talk to my husband about it. I had to be mercilessly honest and add the necessary drama, so this time, it was obvious to him how serious I was. How bad I felt. And this has been going on for months. No, actually, for years. I wanted to make it clear to him that we had to change something because it was no longer fun the way it was. That my emotional state was completely unacceptable. That I was now more willing to live on a minimum wage and, if necessary, move into a studio apartment with four people than to continue like this for even a single day.

My husband understood. He knew as well as I did that the working-for-money principle was no longer satisfactory for us. It was precisely this working model that had brought me into this unbearable situation. Because if I didn't work, I didn't earn anything. So I pretty much just worked. I was self-employed, as the term suggests: doing everything my-self, all the time.

My husband then told me about Amazon FBA, a business model in which you buy and sell products under your own brand on Amazon. I liked the idea. It sounded simple; I could work alone and regardless of location. Plus, I would make almost passive income once the business was set up. Amazon FBA sounded like the solution to all my problems, so shortly after, I attended a seminar to learn all about it.

How Do I Simplify My Life?

Over the next six months, I worked harder than ever as I built my Amazon business, specifically my Amazon USA business, because, as a Swiss citizen, it was easier for me to do business in the USA than in Europe. One disadvantage was that I had to do everything in English, not my native language. But at the end of the day, it was still the lesser evil than dealing with the dreadful European bureaucracy.

The last month of spring had just begun, and my joy was boundless: my product was purchased for the first time on May 2nd. Bring on the champagne! It actually worked! I was finally compensated for the effort and nerves I had invested.

At this point, I won't go into details about the problems I previously faced, how much I had to organize and find answers on Google and YouTube, and what nerves the company Amazon itself cost me. It would make its own book. A drama in seven acts. Nevertheless, I kept going, stuck with it, and didn't give up because I was sure the Amazon business would be my ticket to freedom. The prospect of a freer life and more time with my family motivated me to start all over again. To do this, I was prepared to take a chance, take a financial risk, and familiarize myself with an unknown topic.

However, that also meant that in addition to my tasks as a millionaire manager, the Tesla rental service, and being a mom, I now also had to navigate my Amazon team: the manufacturer in China, the illustrator in Ukraine, the Amazon account manager in Pakistan, my two interim storage facilities in the USA, and the freight forwarder in Switzerland – all in different time zones and with different cultural working methods. And, of course, new difficulties arose all the time.

At first, there was no more air freight because only a few planes took off due to the pandemic. So I had to switch to sea freight, and the goods took much longer to arrive in the USA. Of course, I wasn't the only one with this problem, and the fight for a place on the vessel began. Prices quadrupled, and freight containers became scarce. Then, American customs reported that the goods had been declared too late, and a fine was due. It was like the precipice to Amazon hell!

With every new hurdle that came my way, my motivation and confidence in making this business a success waned. Financial worries began to cause me increasing concern. While I reliably paid all my freelancers and suppliers, nothing was left for my company. I seriously asked myself why I was doing all this to myself.

While I increasingly doubted myself and my economic abilities, the test report from my quality manager in China hit me like a drama of epic proportions: Of the 2,000 items produced, just 800 were in sellable condition. The rest had serious defects. The condition of the goods was far from the quality I wanted to offer my customers.

The problems around me seemed to pelted down on me like unrelenting bombardment. The shelling reached such intensity that I no longer felt able to defend myself. My strength was exhausted, and the inevitable happened: I collapsed – not physically, but on a much deeper, spiritual level. The constant confrontation with new problems had left its mark.

One morning, I was no longer able to enter my office. Just thinking about it made me sick. My heart was pounding increasingly harder, and my body was shaking. I was terrified that I would face more problems if I opened my notebook. The enormous stress, the indescribable pressure! I felt like I had been hit by a freight train and slammed into the ground by a steamroller.

There I sat, a shaky, sweaty heap of misery, afraid of a notebook. And exactly at that moment, it was there again, this irrepressible longing for a simple life! An uncomplicated, easy life without mile-long to-do lists, problems, and resistance that I had to eliminate.

After I had treated myself to a fag and – under these circumstances – a decaffeinated espresso, at least my sweats had subsided. I knew I had to act now. I reached for my cell phone. 'How do I simplify my life?' I typed into the search form with limp fingers. And Google showed me a book called "Simplify Your Life." The book's authors, Werner Tiki Küstenmacher and Lothar Seiwert, describe how you can simplify various areas of your life and regain more clarity in an opaque mess. My curiosity was piqued, and at the same time, a small glimmer of hope flared up in me. Was this book the key to escaping my personal nightmare?

I ordered the book, and it only took me two days to read it from beginning to end, which was remarkable. Because usually, I don't read books. I want to write them myself. However, here, I made an exception. The book not only covered simple decluttering but was a source of inspiration on how to simplify your life on every level. Each page was a small revelation, and with each chapter I read, my attitude toward my possessions changed a little more. Although I was known among my family and friends to have a penchant for tidying, sorting, and decluttering, I realized that I hadn't even begun to get rid of all my junk and clutter. Of course, disposing of broken plant pots or old toys was easy. When we moved out of our large four-story house three years earlier to live in a smaller ground-floor rental apartment, I had sorted out so many things that poor Toni – a family friend and second-hand goods dealer – drove his van a total of seven times back and forth to cart away all our discarded stuff. But objects that had sentimental value and thus held me in the past were a completely different story. The information and explanations in the "Simplify" book made me let go of my tense idea that I absolutely had to keep certain things.

In my case, for example, I kept various exhibits from previous employers in the cupboards and drawers in my office. I had always been proud to have worked for these companies and felt a strong loyalty to them – one of the Big Four accounting firms, a major Swiss bank, the Swiss Ice Hockey Association. I still had a lot of accessories from my time with the Ice Hockey Association, such as pennants, ice hockey sticks with player signatures, address books, stickers, and much more. It was precisely these objects that I had brought with me every time I moved – not because I needed them but because I wanted to avoid dealing with them. I knew I would have to make tough choices if I did because all these objects represented my previous life and were kind of beloved status symbols for everything I had achieved so far. Even though they no longer had any meaning in my current life, I couldn't and didn't want to part with them.

However, I increasingly asked myself to whom these things were supposed to prove something. My kids? Probably not. It's very likely in the nature of children that they don't find anything cool that their parents do or have done in the past. My two boys were no exception. Even if I had trashed hotel rooms with Guns' n' Roses in the '90s or rapped with Snoop Dogg on the hood of his lowrider gangster car, they wouldn't care in the slightest. And after thirteen years of marriage, my husband knew me well enough that his image of me would not change because of previous successes.

I gradually realized that these dusty artifacts were tying me to days long gone and that it was now time to let go of the past. I entered my office, opened the drawer, and hesitantly picked up the first item. It was a puck with the logo of the U-18 Ice Hockey World Championship that had taken place in Switzerland. At that time, I was able to present the silver medals to the Russian ice hockey team together with the city president. I couldn't help but grin. I remembered only too well standing in awe in front of the burly two-meter Russians and holding the shiny plate with the medals on it in my hands. Since this experience was obviously still very fresh in my memory and I also had a photo of it, I put the ice hockey puck in the 'Toni box,' as well as all the other ice hockey pucks from various NHL hockey teams, ice hockey stickers, and car pennants. I also let go of a laptop bag, a ballpoint pen, a notepad from the accounting firm, an agenda, and a backpack from the bank. With each ex-employer status symbol that I discarded, I felt prouder and more liberated – proud that I had finally faced these uncomfortable decisions and liberated because I could let things go. In the end, there was still a watch with my name engraved on it, which I had received from the bank when I passed my final apprenticeship exam. I also kept a golden shoehorn, which was also an award. However, it was only allowed to stay for practical reasons, not sentimental ones.

My sense of achievement inspired me. I had finally removed this gigantic colossus from my life, consisting of a hodgepodge of bygone eras! I wanted more of this feeling, so I immediately took on the next difficult task: letters and cards.

There was a huge plastic box in the basement where I kept every congratulations card, birth announcement, wedding card, greeting card, and letter. All these years, I didn't want to decide what to do with it. And I got an uneasy feeling with every new card that disappeared into it. Even though it languished in various basements for years, this box bothered me enormously. But just thinking about throwing the cards and letters in the trash made me feel guilty. Bad karma, I thought. That's why I never wanted to deal with it.

But now I felt encouraged by my sense of success, and I thought my karma couldn't get any worse anyway. Now, the time was right to finally tackle this challenge. So I brought the monster up from the basement.

I sat on my office floor for an entire Sunday and read every single letter and card. It was funny, sad, amusing, and depressing. While reading, I found myself in a completely different world – one that was long gone. I felt overwhelmed when I put the last letter back in its envelope. But at least I now knew that almost everything in this box was allowed to go except for four letters that touched me and that I, therefore, wanted to have in my life for a little while longer.

I didn't want to keep the rest. I gave myself permission not to have to feel guilty about the people who wrote me the letters and cards. Because the memories and gratitude are not necessarily tied to material objects and are far better off in my heart than in a musty basement.

Sentimental Stuff: Status Symbols, Heirlooms, Gifts, Letters, Keepsakes

If you're also in the mood to get rid of your sentimental junk, here's a guide on how to get started. Basically, you can always follow the same pattern, regardless of whether you're decluttering souvenirs, heirlooms, status symbols, or personal letters.

Step 1: Get Started

If you'd like to start but just don't know where to start because you can't see the stuff because of all the possessions, just take the first decisive step. I deliberately never imagined the whole thing but started with the smallest possible action, such as emptying out the drawer in which I kept various memorabilia. Just start, it's easy.

Step 2: Be Prepared

Luckily, I always had my 'Toni box' handy. It's best to take a basket or cardboard box to place the discarded items into.

Step 3: Go the Extra Mile

To be successful in decluttering, it's important always to clear out all items in the category you want to declutter from the drawer, dresser, or closet. This is the only way to get an overview of what you own.

Step 4: Be Honest

It's helpful to pick up each item individually and ask yourself if it makes you happy or if it's really needed. If the answer is yes, feel free to keep it. However, if you feel uncomfortable or never use the item, it's time to let it go.

Step 5: Getting It Out of the House

Once you're done decluttering, getting the discarded stuff out of the house as soon as possible is important. You can get rid of them in several ways, such as recycling, donating, giving away, or selling. However, it is important not to hold on to a certain price doggedly when selling. You're just wasting time unnecessarily. We often have unrealistic ideas about the value of our items that the market is unwilling to pay. Even if you only receive a small amount for your discarded items, it's better than leaving them lying around unused. In the best case, someone else will find joy in it.

EXTRA TIP: I invested the proceeds of my sold stuff in an ETF. Compared to a bank account, where my money is exposed to inflation and doesn't earn interest, ETFs have historically performed better over a longer period of time. Or maybe you have a special love for a specific company? Then, you could treat yourself to shares with the proceeds from the sale. I, for one, couldn't live with not owning Starbucks stock.

Here you will find a little inspiration on what you could declutter in the category "Sentimental Stuff":

☐ Heirlooms that have no emotional value or even make you sad

☐ Gifts you don't like, don't need, or that don't bring you joy

☐ Status symbols such as trophies, medals, statues, or gifts from former employers

☐ Souvenirs and keepsakes such as shells or sand from your vacation

☐ Key chains, stickers, pennants, drawings, etc.

☐ Letters, postcards, and greeting cards

EXTRA TIP: It can be helpful to create a beautiful memory box that can hold sentimental or curious items. Instead of piling a thousand things somewhere in the basement, consciously selected favorite pieces can bring great joy. When the box is full, it's time to let go of something or add nothing more. This will ensure that you only keep the things that are really close to your heart. At the same time, you avoid accumulating too much insignificant stuff again.

Multiple Jobs. No Vacation. No Time for Family. Zero Francs Profit.

Six months had passed again, and the first trees were already shedding their colorful leaves. Nature may have changed, but my status quo remained the same. I still had too many obligations and could only take care of the most urgent ones. There was also the sale of our house. This wasn't planned, but after our tenants unexpectedly terminated the lease, we quickly decided to sell it.

Of course, we were a little emotional at the beginning. Thirteen years ago, when we were not yet thirty, we felt very lucky to buy our own home. But a lot has changed since then.

Of course, it didn't take long for those around us to show their lack of understanding: "You don't just sell your house! After all, there is no better investment than your own four walls. And what about your children if they want to live in this house one day?" I could list countless such objections that we had to listen to. Except for our closest family members, we refrained from giving long explanations.

A home that you live in is not an investment. Especially not when you had to go into debt to your last pair of underwear to do it. Seen in this way, we lived in our assets, which were, in reality, a liability and worked absolutely not for us but against us. A liability that constantly wanted to be nurtured and cared for, a liability into which we invested even more assets in the form of renovations, garden design, new equipment, and so on. We also knew for a long time that we neither wanted nor needed that much space. We didn't plan to live in the same house and place until the end of our days – we wanted to be free and flexible. And no, we didn't have a guilty conscience because – in an utterly un-Swiss way – we wouldn't be able to pass on a house to our children in forty years that they would probably never want to live in themselves.

Nevertheless, we had many fond memories of this house. Before we moved in, together with my parents, we had been working on it for weeks. Our two boys had grown up in these four walls, taken their first steps, spoken their first words, and done a lot of nonsense. But in the end, it was just a house – stones, walls, and bricks. We felt at home anywhere the four of us could be together.

We also discussed the planned sale with our boys. They saw it pragmatically. And since none of the four of us could imagine ever moving in there again, our decision was made. We sold the house to a lovely family three months later and felt light and free. Another one less obligation that we had to think and worry about. The sale proceeds also finally allowed us to put the money to work for us. In this way, we could lay the foundation for later passive income.

Meanwhile, I was still researching the topics of 'time management' and 'increasing productivity.' I tried to introduce routines and tried the Eisenhower Matrix, the Pareto Principle, time blocking, focus times, and several other methods. Unfortunately, very few techniques made sense to me and, therefore, did not improve my efficiency. And somehow, I didn't feel at all comfortable with this self-optimization mania. Everything was aimed at 'faster, better, and more.' But my goal was in the opposite direction: 'slower, more mindful, and less.' It seemed hopeless.

Four sleepless nights later, during which my old friend – fear paranoia – was happily busy imagining 111 horror scenarios of what bad things could happen to my family, I was lying sluggishly on the sofa. I procrastinated to perfection because I couldn't decide what to start with because of all the to-dos, so I didn't do anything. I lay in my personal 'place to be' and scrolled through Instagram. I read a sentence on one of my feel-good accounts that immediately captivated me. I intuitively knew it would be a life-changer!

"My goal is no longer to get more done
but rather to have less to do."

– Francine Jay –

This core idea is as simple as it is ingenious! It gave me a new perspective from which I had never looked at the whole thing before. But it made sense! Until now, I had desperately tried to sort, prioritize, manage, and work through my numerous to-dos. And no matter what self-optimization technique I used, my to-do list was still endless at the end of the day. It never occurred to me to ensure I didn't have so much to do in the first place.

I immediately started thinking about what tasks I could get rid of. I didn't take long to realize what should best disappear immediately: The Tesla rental service. This business was extremely time-consuming because it required a lot of personal effort for both my husband and me. Just cleaning the Teslas was very time-consuming. There were also countless invoices, inquiries, emails, and management tasks for social media accounts. Sure, the income was good – but was it good enough to justify the enormous amount of work?

Next, I thought about my clients. I loved my clients and felt very connected to them. But did I still love the work? If I was honest, the answer was clearly no. Most of the time, I couldn't work as efficiently as I would like because I lacked answers and information from my clients. As a result, I had a whole board full of 'waiting for' tasks. This circumstance had bothered me for a long time and became increasingly stressful because the to-dos constantly buzzed through my mind, but I couldn't finish them and cross them off my list. In addition, there were all the recurring tasks, such as expense reports and accounting. All this combined left me feeling like I could never get anything done, let alone manage the various commitments. I slowly realized this was a major factor in feeling so overwhelmed and burned out.

So, it was obvious to me that I had to give up my clients if I wanted to improve my situation in the long term. But thinking about it almost broke my heart. All my clients have been loyal to me since I started my business. They were my babies. Would I really have the heart to let them go?

The Amazon business was very capital-intensive and highly unpredictable. I had to react to many factors that were beyond my control. It also continually presented me with new problems that wore me down. However, I also knew that once the business was up and running, it would give me an almost passive income. I wasn't ready to give up yet.

Aside from my professional obligations, I knew I also needed to clear out my personal life. I wanted to eliminate everything that stressed me out, didn't bring me joy, or was too inconvenient. I had already taken the first step by starting to clear out emotional garbage and status symbols. My goal was to clean out the entire apartment, every single room. So there was still a lot to do.

I also decided not to host any more children's birthday parties from now on. I hated it! The invitations, the preparations, and then the hustle and bustle of all the strange children in the house... But what I hated most was that I couldn't even look forward to my own children's birthdays. Because of these other children's parties, I experienced this horror in my mind's eye already weeks before. So, get rid of them! From now on, we will take the children out of school on their birthdays and spend the day as each birthday child wants. I also refused to bake for school events in the future. I brought chips or drinks. Basta! I also canceled all events I didn't want to attend and meetings with people who negatively influenced my peace of mind.

I realized that I also had to simplify certain everyday processes. For example, I decided to reintroduce a weekly menu plan. This way, I would avoid pointless wasting time and be more organized in the kitchen. I also had to find a solution for the pan lids flying around. And the mother of all classics: I no longer wanted to stand in front of a bulging closet for hours and still have no idea what to wear.

So, my plan was clear, and I was actually ready for battle in my combat boots. But first, I had to talk to my husband about the Tesla rental service. I was dreading that because this business was, first and foremost, his baby. But I couldn't avoid this discussion if we really wanted to change something. But not without coffee. And then close your eyes and hope for the best. Or rather, open your eyes because we looked closely at the business figures. And we experienced the shock of our lives! The income was good as expected, but since we constantly invested in the IT infrastructure and inventory, the bottom line was that we were left with a giant zero. It laughed maliciously at us and clearly showed us what we could do with our profit.

We were stunned! We both worked like crazy. Together, we had five jobs, forgo vacations, hardly had a free weekend, and had too little time for the family. And now all this hard work isn't even worth it financially?!

I looked at my husband in horror and asked, "What the hell are we doing here?!" He just shook his head in consternation, and I think that was the first time he really started to think about it. Apparently, we had gotten terribly lost somewhere.

After a while, he raised his head, looked at me, and surprisingly said: "The Tesla rental service company can go." At first, I was speechless. But then I cheered. Internally. I knew how difficult this decision must be for him. Nevertheless, a weight fell off my chest, and it was precisely at that moment that I decided to let my clients go, too. I actually knew it months ago. This step was inevitable if I wanted to escape my hamster wheel and give my life a different direction. As the saying goes, new things can only come when old things go. And I think it's right.

We didn't wait long to put our plans into action. In the following weeks, while my husband organized the sale of the Tesla rental service and terminated the rental agreement for the Tesla rental premises, I gave notice to my clients. And that was one of the hardest things I've had to do in my life so far. I tried really hard to approach it objectively and take businessmen as a good example. I said to myself, "This is business. Would a man make such a fuss? There would be nothing about my babies or whiny hesitations!" So it shouldn't be a problem since I didn't fit the typical image of a woman anyway, neither in my thoughts nor in my actions. But in business matters, of all things, the female species prevailed.

I informed my clients in a womanly manner: in long conversations about what a man would have said in one sentence. Afterward, I cried into my pillow and doubted my decision. But then, as the bitter taste of my guilty conscience slowly faded, relief finally set in. I was happy about my decision and pushed forward with the dossier handovers.

At the same time, I continued to act as a problem solver in Amazon hell. And there really was no shortage of issues.

Because my previous producer manufactured my products with subpar quality, I had to look for a new one. On top of that, due to the strict Covid rules in China, manufacturers needed twice as long to manufacture the goods. In addition, the electricity shortage in Asia made production more expensive. Transport costs continued to go through the roof and were many times higher than a year ago. These additional expenses consumed all my profits.

It slowly dawned on me why Amazon YouTubers always said that Amazon was purely a numbers game. I should have calculated more precisely! Or, to be more precise, if I had made any calculations at all, I would have been able to react more flexibly to the new initial situation. But I'll be honest: I just don't care about numbers. Except for the numbers in the form of credits to my account. But of course, they didn't happen. The dollar rolled, but not into my pockets. It's actually almost embarrassing when you think about my job title.

It almost seemed as if, after all these years of dealing with numbers of all kinds, the creative rebel in me now came out and demanded her right to exist. Because the only thing I really enjoyed about the Amazon business was developing beautiful products to offer my customers added value in an aesthetically pleasing way. I managed that really well. However, I had to admit to myself that I was definitely no longer a businesswoman. The woman who once loved meetings in fancy hotels and restaurants in the city and cheekily placed her Chanel purse next to clients' Aston Martin keys was no longer there. I have no idea where she had gone. She probably ran as fast as she could, far, far away. In any case, she was clearly no longer here.

That's why I quickly decided to clear out my closet. Since there was no longer a female boss, I didn't need a hundred thousand business clothes in my wardrobe.

Wardrobe

Decluttering my clothes was definitely the most fun for me because I had a sense of achievement fairly quickly. Presumably, pretty much everyone has some clothes in their closet that they can easily part with.

The first step was to clear everything out. This was important because it was the only way I could see how much I really owned. After that, I took every single piece of clothing in my hand and asked myself the following questions:

1. Do I wear it?
2. Do I like wearing it?
3. Is the size okay?
4. Does it fit my current lifestyle?
5. Would I buy it again?

If I answered no to just one of these questions, the piece was ready to go. Unfortunately, sometimes, the answer was not so simple. That's why I soon had amassed a considerable 'I don't know' pile. This was the trickiest of all. All the clothes that I hadn't worn once ended up in this pile, either because there had never been the right occasion for them or because I didn't like wearing them. It was even more difficult for me to give them away if they had been expensive. However, I had to admit to myself that the money for it had long since been spent.

I tried to sell top-brand clothes. However, I quickly had to say goodbye to profit expectations that were too high. Even my Chanel coat could not be sold by the classy second-hand shop after a year. And my Gucci purse, for which I had once paid 3,400 euros in Monaco, finally found a new owner for 300 francs. It was sad, but there was no point in complaining. That's why I said to myself: Take the money and run! Otherwise, in a year's time, I would still have hoarded the pieces in the closet, where they would have subtly made me feel guilty day after day.

Other difficult candidates were dresses in the sense of 'I could still wear this for sports or gardening.' Of course, I also had a subcategory called: 'When I go horseback-riding again.' This department had been around for thirty years. And guess how many times I've been on a horse in the last thirty years. Three times! And one of those times, I wore my wedding dress. So, get rid of it. Even if I planned to get back on a horse in the next thirty years, I'm sure I'd find something suitable to wear.

A little motivation for the difficult cases:

Expensive Clothes / Top-Brand Clothes

Try to sell them. Don't dwell on it too long, though. The money is already gone.

Clothes that are too big / too small

What worked in the past or will work later is not useful in the present. It is important that your clothes fit you NOW and support you in the best possible way today.

Clothes for Gardening, Pottery, etc.

A simple no. (Unless you garden and do pottery regularly).

Torn Clothes

You can repair them or get them repaired. However, this should be done within the next five days. Otherwise, they will still be defective in a year.

Wedding Dress

I gave my wedding dress to the clothing drive. The memory of my wedding day is in my head, not in the dress. Of course, you can also sell, give away, or donate your dress. However, mine was too dirty and torn due to its use on the horse to sell it without a guilty conscience.

Some tips on how to organize your wardrobe in an aesthetic and practical way:

1. Sort clothes: The first step is to sort all the clothes. You can divide them into categories such as sweaters, blouses, pants, dresses, jackets, etc., and then organize them by color.

2. Use matching hangers and other small helpers: If you use uniform hangers, you will achieve a wonderful, harmonious overall look in your closet. For pants, there are extra pants hangers, which are space-saving. Shower curtain rings are ideal for neatly hanging scarves and other accessories.

3. Use drawer organizers: They help you keep your clothes neat and organized. You can store your socks, underwear, accessories, etc. in different compartments.

4. Use transparent shoe boxes: Shoes can be stored in stackable boxes in the closet. You can keep track of everything, and your shoes will be neatly stored.

5. Create visibility: If you can see your clothes and they're neatly stored, you'll be more likely to wear them. If you hide things, you're more likely to forget them.

6. Invest in lighting: Good light can help make your wardrobe look aesthetically pleasing and give you a

better view of your wardrobe. For example, you could install LED strips.

Don't stress if you can't get rid of all your excess clothes right away. It's okay if it takes a little longer. I have cleaned out my closet several times, and each time, it was easier for me to say goodbye to even the more difficult pieces.

After my last decluttering action, I created a capsule wardrobe for myself. I've wanted to do this for a long time, but an idiosyncratic character trait stood in my way: I hardly ever wore my favorite clothes. It was the same with other objects that I liked: I stored them carefully without ever using them. Whether candles, pens, or even notebooks, I regretted using them. In my memory box, I actually found stickers from the eighties that I had collected in first grade. They were my holy grail at the time. But instead of enjoying them or sticking them somewhere where I could have seen them every day and enjoyed them, they languished their existence in a box. And now, almost forty years later, they have no use or emotional value to me. That really got me thinking. Actually, life was too short not to use and enjoy the beautiful things. So I decided to put on my favorite clothes, light the gorgeous candles, and fill up the lovely notebooks. This decision helped me to finally say goodbye to the dresses in the category 'I could wear them for riding, gardening, or cooking' and paved the way for my capsule wardrobe.

This proved to be another milestone towards a simpler life. From now on, I knew that everything I chose from my wardrobe would fit in size, look great, and be comfortable to wear because I arranged my wardrobe exactly that way.

Capsule Wardrobe

What Is a Capsule Wardrobe?

It's a minimalist wardrobe comprising just your favorite, basic, and necessary pieces.

What Is the Goal of a Capsule Wardrobe?

All items of clothing in the closet should be combinable with each other. This means you can still create many different looks with just a few pieces and accessories.

How Does the Capsule Wardrobe Work?

It is crucial that you first determine a color concept. This ensures that all pieces can be combined with each other. The problem with a conventional wardrobe is that everything is hanging topsy-turvy. Then you stand in front of the closet and spend ages thinking about what to wear because you constantly have to figure out which pieces you can combine. With a capsule wardrobe, on the other hand, every piece of clothing goes with everything else, and it only consists of your favorites. So you can just reach in and get what you feel like.

What Is the Benefit of a Capsule Wardrobe?

First, you don't waste time thinking about what to wear. Second, you need significantly fewer clothes and use them more consciously. Third, your closet is much tidier and cleaner. Fourth, you prevent impulse purchases because you follow a precise pattern. You know what you already have and what color palette a new piece of clothing should fit into. If you are still missing a specific piece, search specifically for it.

All my clothing (including my jackets, hats, gloves, scarves, and shoes) is beige, rose, white, gray, and black. All colors match and go well together. Plus, all the pieces are made from a material I like to wear. They fit perfectly in size and support my current lifestyle.

Shoes

Sorting shoes can be challenging. Women often own many pairs that go with different outfits. This was especially noticeable to me when packing for vacation, as I needed a whole suitcase for my shoes.

I wanted to reduce my huge collection. So, I thought about which shoes I could part with the easiest. The first thing I did was weed out all the pairs I couldn't walk in elegantly, followed by the ones I hadn't worn in the last two years. Even shoes that were too small or too big had to go. I also gave away two out of three pairs of flip-flops. Ultimately, I still had more shoes than I would have liked. However, I let it go for the moment and planned to take stock again in a few months.

Which shoes to get rid of? A small selection:

☐ Pumps and high heels

☐ Boots and ankle boots

☐ Ballerinas

☐ Sandals

☐ Flip-flops

☐ Winter shoes

☐ Slippers

☐ Sneakers

EXTRA TIP: Since all the shoes are neatly lined up after decluttering, now would be an ideal time to pamper them (clean, polish, and impregnate).

Accessories

Afterward, I took care of my bags, belts, shawls, and other accessories. In this area, a lot of unnecessary stuff had also accumulated. I definitely had no use for six pairs of sunglasses and fifteen belts. In the end, I kept two pairs of sunglasses, a belt, and a foulard.

Sorting out accessories – a little suggestion:

□ Belt

□ Foulards and scarf

□ Sunglasses

□ Hats, baseball caps

□ Handbags

□ Travel bags, sports bags, backpacks, belt bags

□ Wallets

Jewelry

Although I had a large collection of necklaces, rings, and bangles, I usually only wore them to client appointments – and always the same pieces. To make my life a little easier again, I checked each piece of jewelry individually and wondered if I still liked it. This saved me from making future decisions.

Ultimately, I kept only a few selected pieces: a necklace, two watches, two rings, and a bracelet. Everything else was allowed to go with Toni, regardless of whether it was real or costume jewelry. I just didn't have time to sell the stuff, and it made me happy that I was able to support Toni and his small business through it.

You could look through the following pieces of jewelry:

☐ Earrings

☐ Necklaces

☐ Bracelets

☐ Watches

☐ Rings

☐ Piercings

☐ Brooches

☐ Pendants

I put all the clothes, shoes, and accessories that were allowed to stay back in the closet. From now on, I will be dressed in no time! I would have loved to have a look at it every ten minutes because the sight of my half-empty closet so enchanted me. (Writes the woman who once owned a dressing room the size of an art gallery.) My husband came up curiously and looked inside as well because he wondered what made his wife so happy. But when he saw the result of my decluttering, all that came out of his mouth was a stunned "Where are all your clothes, honey?" Well, they were in the sixteen trash bags, which didn't even fit into the used clothes container. Apart from that, downsizing would-n't have hurt his half of the closet either. I don't know how many shirts a man needs in his lifetime, but I'm sure 52 is too many. Unfortunately, the decluttering virus had not yet jumped to my husband.

I, on the other hand, was just getting started. With the coffee cup in my hand and a lot of enthusiasm, I roamed through our living room. Like a tigress on the hunt, I was on the lookout for things to declutter next.

The Living Room

I calmly looked around the room. Anything that bothered me or didn't bring me joy had to go. Items that didn't belong in our living room were placed in a suitable location. I cleaned out all the cabinets and drawers and removed un-necessary decorations. After that, no more objects were in the living room that did not serve a certain purpose. I only put up seasonal decorations in autumn and at Christmas time. In spring, bouquets of tulips, which I treat myself to purposefully and consciously, are the only decoration in the room. A picture frame with a photo of our boys and some photo books adorn our country house closet all year round.

Some ideas on what to declutter in the living room:

☐ Unused tablecloths

☐ Furniture

☐ Lamps

☐ Mirror

☐ Clocks

☐ Decorative pillows, throw blankets, plush toys, dolls

☐ Carpets

☐ Plants

☐ Art objects that don't appeal to you (anymore)

☐ Craft and hobby materials

☐ Burnt-down candles

☐ Promotional gifts (pens, pocketknives, etc.)

☐ Unnecessary decorative items

DVDs and CDs

Since we only downloaded or streamed movies via the well-known services, it quickly became clear that we wanted to part with the three moving boxes full of DVDs and VHS tapes. We didn't have a working player anyway. CDs were also redundant as we listened to music via Spotify and Sonos.

The following relics from the last century could be given away:

☐ DVDs

☐ CDs

☐ VHS tapes

☐ Cassettes

☐ Vinyl

EXTRA TIP: You could organize your music on Spotify or Sonos. The choice is limitless and doesn't take up any space whatsoever. I created playlists for all seasons and moods, whether cozy autumn jazz music, happy Christmas carols, mood boosters for the January low, or summer country music.

TV

Decluttering the TV? Yes, exactly! I did it by creating a personalized list that included only my favorite channels. I put the most frequently watched programs at the beginning, and I summarized similar channels. My husband did the same based on his male preferences. Then, I looked through all our recordings, sorted them out, and archived the shows I wanted to keep. Although it took a little effort, the result was worth it. No more endless zapping through eight hundred and thirty-two TV channels!

Step by step to a decluttered TV:

1. Delete channels you never watch
2. Create a channel list based on personal preferences
3. View, delete, and archive recordings
4. Check series recordings and keep them if necessary
5. Review and clean up the archive

Magazines / Recipes

This was a difficult topic! I collected old magazines for years and kept them under our coffee table. However, I only kept them because of individual articles that interested me. Sometimes, I used them as a source of inspiration for garden design or kept them just because of one exciting post. I kept all the autumn and Christmas issues anyway because I loved the covers – and because they smelled so delicious!

My husband and children couldn't help but laugh when I sometimes sniffed at the magazines and sighed contentedly.

Nevertheless, I decided to let go of the magazines and not buy any new ones. I found them quite expensive, and I could discover the same content on Instagram or Pinterest. I could have stored the torn pages and article snippets in an old-school folder, just as a digital solution such as 'Evernote' or the note app on your mobile phone would have been an option. But I had decided: sniff them one last time – and goodbye.

My recipe collection was another story. Although I had already filed all the recipes by category in a folder, I never looked at it because it was neither practical nor attractively designed. So, I decided to look through all the recipes and save only the ones in my recipe app, which had a realistic chance that I would want to cook or bake them one day. I did the same with my cookbooks.

If you don't like saving digitally, you could alternatively create a nice recipe book or index cards. Personally, I prefer a digital setup—mainly because of the convenient meal planning feature. Thanks to my saved lunch and dinner ideas, I now have a great selection of go-to meals. There are also simple tools that let you manage recipes and create shopping lists with ease—no fuss at all.

You could browse through the following printed objects, digitize them and, if necessary, dispose of them:

☐ Magazines

☐ Collection of recipes

☐ Newspapers

☐ Cookbooks

☐ Brochures and flyers

Books

One of my all-time favorite things was going to bookstores with my firstborn. We strolled through the shop, enjoyed the cozy atmosphere, and browsed through the books and displays. We often left the store with one or more new books. Unfortunately, they lost their appeal as soon as they arrived at our home. They would then lie around in the living or bedroom for weeks and finally end up unread on the bookshelf in the office.

But that was about to change! I took all the books from my shelf and asked myself for each one:

- Do I want to read it next?
- Would I read it again?
- Is the content still relevant and up-to-date?
- Does it bring me joy?

Ultimately, I kept six special books that inspired me in different ways: 'Rich Dad, Poor Dad' by Robert Kiyosaki because you just can't read this book often enough. 'Atomic Habits' by James Clear because it provides many new insights. 'I Love Christmas in New York' by Langenscheidt because there is simply nothing better than Christmas in New York! 'Homebody' by Joanna Gaines because I love the show 'Fixer Upper.' And two books by illustrator Megan Hess that just make me incredibly happy.

A pleasant side effect of this action is that I haven't made any impulse purchases since then. Instead, I'm already thinking about whether the book should be placed next to my other six books and whether there was a real chance I would read it.

For more clarity on the shelf: You could look through these books again – and if you don't want to read them a second time or the content is no longer up-to-date, get rid of them:

☐ Novels

☐ Biographies

☐ Non-fiction books

☐ Travel guide

☐ School and study books

☐ Law books

☐ Duden

☐ Dictionaries

☐ Encyclopedias

☐ Picture books

☐ Cookbooks

EXTRA TIP: Sort your books by color. It's an appealing way to make your bookshelf look calmer.

Out of the House and Out of Your Mind

Warm Christmas lights and colorful decorations shone everywhere, creating a festive atmosphere. Magnificent Advent wreaths adorned the doors of the houses, and the streetlamps had festive bows. A hint of cinnamon and pine scent was in the air. At home, my Christmas playlist played on an endless loop and accompanied me from early in the morning until late at night. Every note increased my anticipation of Christmas, and I enjoyed every minute of the cozy Advent season.

Unfortunately, in recent years, I haven't been able to enjoy my beloved pre-Christmas season as much as I would have liked. Just before the end of the year, I always had a lot of work for my clients and, therefore, often had little time left for all the Christmas activities I would have liked to celebrate with my family – unless I had started them in September. However, with the sunshine and late summer temperatures, I couldn't get into the Christmas spirit by any stretch of the imagination.

This year, everything was different. After handing over most of the client dossiers to my successors, I finally had time for all the wonderful pre-Christmas activities I had always longed for. Together with my husband and our children, I visited Christmas markets, baked delicious cookies, and watched Christmas movies. The highlight of the Advent season was a family trip, including grandma, to a farmer in the village to choose the Christmas tree. Half the town met there and enjoyed the cozy Christmas atmosphere with a glass of mulled wine.

My life was too demanding, complicated, and stressful when I started this journey. I had learned that letting go was the answer to much of what I was looking for: less stress, less distraction from what was important, and less stuff to manage. The richness of letting go for me was that I had more time for the things that were important to me. I increasingly had the feeling that I was regaining control over my actions. The more discarded items and professional obligations left my life, the more I saw of my new life. And the easier my life became, the happier we all became.

While getting rid of things, topics such as 'gratitude,' 'mindfulness,' and 'slow living' came more and more into focus. Suddenly, I felt gratitude for the things I had. And this gratitude led to more mindfulness. I nurtured and cared for our belongings with more care. I increasingly questioned what we were buying and how and where the goods were made. As a result of this, I began to wonder more and more whether my Amazon business could still be reconciled with my values.

The more free time I had, the more intensely I felt the slow pace of life. Because I was no longer directed through the day like a puppet by other people and external influences. I learned to enjoy the process, to listen carefully to my children as they told me about their experiences, to listen to the rooster crowing in the early hours of the morning, and to rejoice in how the Moroccan peppermint stoically defied the freezing winter temperatures.

Just before Christmas, we reached another milestone when we signed the contract with the buyer of our Tesla rental service. It was a liberating feeling after we had made a series of difficult decisions over the past few months, which sometimes required more and sometimes less courage. And no one could guarantee whether they were the right ones. But we remembered the principle that nothing was set in stone. Each new day would give us another chance to change our lives when it didn't feel right. We just had to find the courage to live our lives in the best way for our family.

This process sometimes required unconventional decisions that did not correspond to society's expectations. Of course, there were long and uncomprehending faces in our environment because we constantly acted contrary to traditional Swiss norms. It's a wonder we weren't chased out of the village with hayforks and torches. But other people's opinions no longer had any relevance to us. It was the first time in months that I hadn't felt controlled by others. And to maintain this freedom, I was determined to continue our path away from the Swiss mainstream, regardless of what other people said or thought. I was still willing to reduce our standard of living even further than ever again be demoralized by problems and endless to-dos all day long.

Decorations

When it was finally time to decorate the apartment for Christmas, I decided to get all the decorations out of the basement. It was a great opportunity to sort everything through together with my children. There were eight crates that we dragged upstairs. Over the years, so much had accumulated that I couldn't even set or hang it up. The selection was so overwhelming that decorating was no longer fun. In addition, there were also some decorative items that I no longer enjoyed.

Accompanied by Dean Martin's atmospheric Christmas classics, we first arranged everything according to season and theme, letting go of broken or unloved items. It was sometimes difficult for me to decide, especially when my children were emotionally attached to certain objects. Of course, we kept them. To make difficult decisions easier for me, I remembered my new principle: Keep only those items that delight you when you see them and that you would buy again.

In the end, all the decorations fit into two boxes. When we put up our Christmas tree a few days later, we immediately disposed of broken or unloved tree decorations.

You can look through and declutter these decorations:

☐ Spring decorations

☐ Summer decorations

☐ Fall decorations

☐ Winter decorations

☐ Christmas decoration

☐ Christmas tree decorations

☐ Advent calendar

☐ Candles

☐ Fragrance lamps and oils, fragrance sticks and diffusers

☐ Real plants and those made of plastic

☐ Decorations to hang up: pictures, dream catchers, garlands, etc.

☐ Clocks

☐ Bowls and baskets

☐ Glass jars

☐ Small decorative pieces such as crystals, figurines, etc.

☐ Door decoration

☐ Light chains

☐ Decoration for the garden and terrace

EXTRA TIP: To keep the dear light riff-raff in check, you can wind the light chains on empty household rolls. Simply make an incision into the cardboard roll and clamp the end of the chain there to hold it in place.

The Bedroom

When I decided to clean up our bedroom, I initially thought there wasn't much to declutter. However, when I opened the drawers of our dresser, I found many things that I wanted to get rid of. Over time, a lot had also accumulated in the boxes under the bed. I just didn't have it on my radar because it wasn't visible at first glance.

First, I sorted out all the decorative cushions and their covers, as we never used them. Spare sheets, linen sheets, and flannel covers were also allowed to go. We have always used the same bed linen for years while the rest of the covers remained untouched. So, it was unlikely that we would need them in the next few years.

In a box under the bed, I found some scraps of fabric that my firstborn had used years ago for handicrafts. Since he had long since outgrown his crafting age and I couldn't sew, I discarded them as well.

Here are some ideas on what you could look through and declutter in the bedroom:

☐ Nightstand drawers

☐ Dressers

☐ Bed linens

☐ Pillows and covers

☐ Blankets

☐ Sheets

☐ Flannel covers

The Bathroom

Decluttering the bathroom is a rewarding category because there is an incredible amount of potential here if you want to get rid of unnecessary things. For me, the topics of 'less waste' and 'sustainability' were getting louder and louder, and that's why I was particularly looking forward to making tabula rasa in the bathroom! I couldn't wait to use up all the shampoos, shower gels, and liquid hand soaps to replace them with eco-friendly products as soon as possible.

Our first step towards sustainability and waste avoidance was to buy plastic-free cotton swabs. I also got washable bamboo make-up remover wipes and soaps from local certi-fied organic producers. We've tried some eco-friendly prod-ucts; some things didn't work for us, but we liked many things, for example, our new towels made of pure organic material. Because they were quite expensive, it was a good time to consider how many hand and bath towels we actually needed. Until then, we had a considerable hotchpotch of bath towels in all sizes and colors. Ultimately, we decided that four bath towels, two hand towels, and a washcloth were sufficient. And we coped very well with it.

A little inspiration for decluttering the bathroom:
- □ Hand and bath towels
- □ Washcloths
- □ Bathrobes
- □ Skin care products such as face creams, masks, etc.
- □ Shower gels, body lotions, and hand and foot creams
- □ Deodorants and perfumes
- □ Hair care products: shampoo, conditioner, hairsprays
- □ Hair accessories such as hair clips, elastics, bands, etc.
- □ Hair dryer, straightener, curling iron, curler, etc.
- □ Combs and brushes
- □ Cosmetics, make-up, brushes, and sponges
- □ Nail polishes
- □ Samples from the pharmacy
- □ Bath toys

EXTRA TIP: Baskets and boxes made of natural materials, such as wood, are a nice way to organize bath utensils and cosmetic products neatly and uncluttered. Drawer organizers are almost indispensable for creating uncluttered order in the cabinets.

The Simple Life Within Reach

Apart from a Zoom call with my freight forwarder on Christmas Eve, the festive season was very relaxed. This was not least due to the pandemic and the associated restrictions. All Christmas parties were canceled, which was a shame, but it also had positive aspects: no business lunches and no hectic driving around to see all sorts of relatives and acquaintances.

That's why we started Christmas morning comfortably with a classic: 'Home Alone.' Later, we strolled through the narrow streets of our picturesque farming village and marveled at the lovingly decorated houses and gardens. The smell of burning firewood added warmth and coziness to the contemplative atmosphere, which I would remember for years to come. My husband and I ended the evening with homemade eggnog.

After New Year's Eve, the festive idyll and blissful eggnog sipping was unfortunately over. My freight forwarder informed me that the ship carrying my goods from China to New York had declared an accident. Information was sparse, and no one knew the consequences. They've never had a case like this before, my freight forwarder told me on the phone, visibly dismayed. Obviously, such an exceptional event happened to me. Sometimes, I really had the feeling that I was a magnet for problems and extraordinary events. In any case, the vessel was damaged, and it was unclear whether my goods would be intact or if they would ever arrive in New York Harbor. Only one thing was sure: if the goods could no longer be saved, this would result in the loss of several tens of thousands of francs.

Just a few months ago, this event would have triggered a psychological meltdown and would have been the starting signal for a panic attack of the highest order. I felt a lot more resilient since I had significantly reduced my obligations and stress levels in the last few months. So this lousy news only cost me a roll of my eyes. Not that it didn't annoy or worry me, but I made a conscious decision to stay calm and deal with the problem if it turned out to be one. Giving up wasn't an option at that point anyway. There was still a tiny chance that the goods would arrive at the Amazon warehouse at some point.

I passed the time waiting with further decluttering activities. Before I wanted to devote myself to the kitchen, a box with receipts and user manuals for various appliances was on the agenda.

User Manuals, Warranties, Receipts

Until now, we have kept all the manuals, receipts, and warranties in a big white box and checked it daily. No, of course not. We didn't look inside once. First, we would have had to search forever for the right receipt, and second, most of them were already so faded that they were barely legible. If we had a question about how to use a device, we did some research on the internet and didn't rummage through that box. That's why I decided to throw all the manuals in the trash. I checked the warranty certificates and receipts to see if we still had the relevant items and if the warranty was still valid.

In the end, I kept only a handful of receipts, which I put in my contract folder. So, we were able to say goodbye to a box again and only kept the really important documents.

Here's how to bring order to your user manuals, warranty certificates, and receipts:

1. First, gather all the user manuals and supporting documents.
2. Check to see if you still own the item.
3. Check if the warranty claim is still valid.
4. Find a home for the leftover receipts and warranty certificates.
5. Everything else goes to the waste paper collection.

EXTRA TIP: If you have an app from the retailer on your phone, you can set receipts and warranty certificates to be stored online only in the app.

Kitchen

My kitchen was a delightful place to declutter! Since cooking is not one of my hobbies, the coffee maker is the only appliance that is really important to me. Basically, I would like to bake, but I always feel extremely stressed by the ingredients. They are then laid crisscrossed and have to be weighed and put together in groups. If you have to separate eggs or – horror upon horror – gelatin comes into play, I'm definitely out. Because I'm overwhelmed, I don't enjoy the whole thing anymore anyway.

And so I got rid of almost all the baking utensils. I only kept a cake pan and the dough scraper. I also discarded the coffee set, as neither my husband nor I drank our coffee from it. We always used the same four coffee cups. We continued with the drinking glasses: We had far too many of them in different designs. I chose the ones I liked best and put the others in the 'Toni box.' After that, I sorted out all the Tupperware containers, bowls, and spatulas. Three whisks were clearly two too many, so only one was allowed to stay. A few days later, I could have used a second one, as I was making two different soups, but I improvised and was determined to make do with what was available to me. The food processor, which had not been used once in the last fifteen years and only took up a lot of space, also had to go.

The wine glasses have been a particular thorn in my side for a long time. We didn't drink wine, so we only took them out of the cupboard when we had guests – which was rare in recent years. Since we agreed that our home had to be furnished for us and not for guests, the wine glasses went into the 'Toni box.' They were followed by two scratched frying pans and a large cooking pot. After that, I sorted out the Christmas cookie molds together with my children. We parted ways with those that didn't give us pleasure or were impractical to handle.

In the end, I put away all the kitchen utensils so that they made our everyday life easier. I placed all the cups, glasses, and plates for my kids so far down that they could easily reach them without having to climb onto the kitchen shelf. I kept all the items we often needed in an easily accessible place. I bought a wooden plate holder at Ikea for the pan lids to keep them neatly in place. So I don't have to put away all the lids first to be able to grab a pan. I have stored the lids of the Tupperware boxes in a small container so that they don't buzz around lost in the cupboard. Since then, I've been able to find every suitable lid immediately.

After arranging the kitchen utensils, I checked all the edibles and spices for their expiration date. I realized that we had too many spices. I gave away the ones we never used and disposed of the ones that were already years past their use-by date.

While cleaning up, I also found paper napkins and placemats. Since they were too good to throw away, I put them at the ready so we could use them instead of paper towels in the near future. After that, we replaced the napkins and paper towels with washable cloth napkins.

A little inspiration on what you could declutter in your kitchen:

☐ Drinking glasses

☐ Wine glasses

☐ Cups

☐ Unused dinnerware

☐ Unused porcelain

☐ Plates

☐ Bowls

☐ Cutlery

☐ Wooden spoons

☐ Toaster, food processor, blender, deep fryer, kettle

☐ Small kitchen utensils such as garlic presses, cheese graters, egg slicers, corkscrews, bottle openers, can openers, etc.

☐ Baking utensils

☐ Cookie molds

☐ Cutting boards

☐ Tupperware

☐ Gratin dish

☐ Pots and pans, incl. lids

☐ Strainers

☐ Baking trays

☐ Edibles

☐ Spices

☐ Tea towels

☐ Napkins

☐ Placemats

☐ Mason jars

☐ Lunch boxes

☐ Coffee-to-go-cups

☐ Water bottles for on-the-go

☐ Thermos bottles and flasks

☐ Unused special tools

EXTRA TIP for a well-organized kitchen:

1. **Decluttering:** Remove all unnecessary items from the kitchen. Give away what is not used or has been sitting around unused for years.

2. **Storage:** Store kitchen utensils and appliances within easy reach. Arrange shelves and cupboards neatly. Use drawer inserts and anti-slip mats to keep everything organized.

3. **Minimalism:** Reduce the number of devices or invest in those that have multiple functions. Only keep devices that you actually need.

4. **Sustainability:** To avoid plastic waste, use eco-friendly alternatives such as cloth napkins, reusable

containers, wooden cutting boards, and beeswax wraps.

5. **Labeling:** Label drawers and bins nicely to make everything easier to find and identify.

6. **Frequently used items close at hand:** Keep frequently used items close to the work surface.

7. **Adorable things for the kitchen:** Treat yourself to beautiful kitchen items such as pretty tea towels, a cute kitchen apron, or tasteful tins. You see these things all day long and should. Therefore, they should radiate joy when you look at them.

8. **Clean out regularly** to keep the kitchen tidy. Go through the cabinets and drawers every few months and remove anything that isn't in use.

Home Office

By now, all my clients were in good hands, and I was able to reduce my office to the essentials.

Due to my affinity for stationery articles, I have amassed an impressive amount of office supplies over the past two decades. I first cleared everything from the cupboards and drawers to get an overview. Although I had a hard time parting with briefcases, folders, registers, sticky notes, and notebooks, I realized that I probably wouldn't live long enough to be able to use them all up. That's why I decided to keep only items that I actually needed in everyday life: my beloved metallic highlighters, some sticky notes, and a few tabs for archiving at the beginning of a new year. And all my pretty notebooks. In return, I only kept one of four cork walls, namely the one that served as a vision board. The other three had previously functioned as to-do lists, which I replaced with a web-based to-do list. Toni picked up the rest.

You could declutter the following items in your home office:

☐ Showcases and Sleeves

☐ Folders

☐ Register

☐ Staplers and staples

☐ Hole puncher

☐ Paper clips

□ Pens, markers, erasers, sharpeners

□ Envelopes and wrappers

□ Sticky notes

□ Seal

□ Stationery

□ Supplies of birthday cards, wedding cards, birth cards, etc.

□ Notebooks

□ Business cards

□ Containers for pens, papers, etc.

□ Miscellaneous snippets and notes

Here are a few ideas for a simple and clear organization of your home office:

1. If you're using **boxes, baskets, and cans**, you can neatly organize pens, markers, sticky notes, and other office supplies in drawers. This helps you find what you need faster and keeps your workspace tidy.

2. **Small drawer boxes** are ideal for storing showcases, envelopes, registers, or documents. To get even more clarity, you can also label them.

3. **To avoid distraction,** the desk should be clean and tidy. You can remove unnecessary things that you

don't need. I went one step further and left my desk completely empty except for my notebook.

4. **To create a calm atmosphere,** folders should have the same type and color throughout and be labeled consistently.

5. **Pretty letter trays or box files** made of cardboard or wood are great for sorting documents that still need to be processed. This way, you can keep track of everything and quickly access important papers.

6. **Marking devices** such as the Brother P-touch or Dymo LabelManager are undoubtedly a good investment. These devices are wonderful helpers for consistently labeling everything – from cans and shelves to folders and containers. They are also used in the kitchen, the workshop, or the garage.

EXTRA TIP: I use the 'Trello' tool to organize my to-dos. It is available on PCs and as an app. With 'Trello,' you can not only create clean to-do lists but also manage entire projects. You can create different boards, move individual cards to other lists, create checklists, insert links, and share them with team or family members.

Personal Documents and Contracts

I created a register folder to organize my personal documents, such as school and work references, the family register, my vaccination card, and other documents. I labeled each register accordingly so I could quickly find what I needed. I used an ordinary ring binder with a register insert and a table of contents for contracts. I also put the handful of receipts and warranties left over from our messy white box in this folder. To make room, I disposed of old application letters, snippets about pension solutions and tax tips, and newspaper articles I could easily find online.

A list of personal documents that should be filed in a well-organized manner:

☐ Birth certificates

☐ Family register

☐ Residence confirmation

☐ Vaccination card and blood group card

☐ School reports

☐ References

☐ Tax returns

☐ Contracts and insurance policies

☐ Passport / ID card

EXTRA TIP: Check your personal documents regularly to ensure they are current. You can also make digital copies and store them on a secure hard drive should you lose your physical documents or they get stolen.

Decluttering Your PC

Quite a lousy crisis! I have to admit that this project definitely didn't exude joy. Not even writing about it exudes joy in any way. But for the sake of completeness, I will force myself to do it anyway. My computer had been disorganized for a long time, as I had been under constant stress for the past few years and often had to save the files quickly without having time for proper sorting. As a result, I created many similar or even identical folders, which led to a complete mess. When I was looking for a specific file, I had to rummage through every folder because I didn't know where I had put what. It was one of the biggest time-wasters in my life. This had to change as soon as possible.

So, I picked myself up and systematically searched through every folder. I deleted unnecessary stuff and renamed files. Where it made sense, I reorganized the folders, merged them, and moved old files to the archive.

Although I was actually more of an analog type and preferred paper, the longer it went on, the more important it became to me to have to store as little as possible physically. On the one hand, to save space and on the other hand, to be flexible in terms of location. That's why I decided to go paperless and gradually switched everything to electronic storage. As a result, I not only had fewer folders on the shelf but also contributed to conserving natural resources. Ultimately, our office was so minimized that we no longer needed one.

Speaking of the electronic office: To create order on the PC, I resorted to the cloud solution 'Dropbox.' I created folders for our family, our company, and a personal folder for myself. Both my husband and I had access to the family and company folders. We organized the folder structure as simply as possible, meaning it had to be straightforward and logical so that we both could easily find our way around it.

Some examples of my folder structure:

Main Folder	Archive
Subfolders	2021
	2020
	and so on
Main Folder	Children
Subfolder	Firstborn
Folders for	School
Folder for	Tennis
	and so on
Subfolder	Secondborn
Folders for	School

Folders for	Soccer
	and so on
Main Folder	Photos
Subfolder	Family
Folders for	2022
Folders for	2021
Subfolder	Vacations
Folder for	Gstaad September 2020
Folder for	New York December 2017
Main Folder	Company XY
Subfolder	Finances
Folders for	Taxes
Folder for	Accounting
Folder for	Accounts payable
Folders for	Accounts receivable
Subfolder	Staff
Folder for	Employee A
Folder for	Employee B
	and so on.

Once you've found a folder structure that's right for you, you'll be able to find the files and information you're looking for quickly and easily in the future.

I used these steps to declutter my PC:

1. Delete, rename, and reorganize files.

2. Create archive folders for old files that need to be kept. Alternatively, you could store old files on an external hard drive or memory stick.

3. Find a straightforward, simple folder structure that makes sense for you and stick to it.

4. Label files so that the date is visible and it is clear which document it is.

5. Move files to their respective folders.

EXTRA TIP: It can be demotivating to imagine having to declutter your entire PC. I've experienced it myself. Tackling only one folder per day or week can help you avoid feeling overwhelmed and get the decluttering process going.

Another suggestion would be to first focus only on the area that causes the most clutter. For example, this could be the downloads folder or the desktop. If you start here, you can quickly delete unnecessary files or move them to appropriate locations to create space and clarity. Once you see progress, moving on to more complex folders often becomes easier.

Email Inbox

Another category I didn't want to do. I knew it would take forever to read through all the emails. However, I was aware of the necessity because I really wanted to have an empty inbox and felt literally crushed by all the emails.

I started by unsubscribing from all incoming newsletters and immediately blocking the senders of unsolicited spam emails. This had the positive effect of reducing my email intake in a very short time. After that, I deleted unnecessary emails and saved important messages as PDFs in the appropriate Dropbox folders. I repeated the same thing with the sent and deleted emails.

I can't put it any other way: It really was a pain in the ass, as my favorite American client always put it so nicely. It was impossible to get this done in one day. I spent about an hour a day reading, deleting, moving, and saving messages. After three weeks, everything was done, and the effort was definitely worth it. My inbox contained only two emails that needed to be processed. It was easy to keep things tidy, if only because I really didn't want to have to do it again!

Here are the simple steps you can take to get your inbox up to speed:

1. Unsubscribe from all newsletters
2. Immediately block spam senders
3. Delete all unnecessary emails
4. Create different folders and move emails

5. Save important emails as PDF files with the print filter 'Microsoft Print to PDF' or via the Outlook function 'Data Files'

6. Keep things tidy by regularly processing incoming emails and tidying up your inbox.

Conventional Mail

Like my online mail, I also wanted to reduce the amount of physically incoming conventional mail in the long term. It was stupid to get the mail out of the mailbox only to throw it in the trash and then have to dispose of it. Therefore, I applied for electronic invoicing wherever possible. When I received magazines from service providers such as health insurance companies, electricity companies, or retailers, I checked their websites to see if I could unsubscribe from the advertising material via an online form. All other advertising letters and catalogs were returned to the sender with the label REFUSE. It was a one-time effort that quickly paid off. Soon, we received only a fraction of the letter mail, and on top of that, we had to dispose of significantly less wastepaper.

With these measures, you can sustainably curb incoming conventional mail:

1. Receive invoices, bank statements, and the like only online

2. 'No advertising and free newspapers' sticker on the mailbox

3. Unsubscribe from newspapers and magazines from health insurance companies, energy suppliers, retailers, etc.

4. Return unsolicited sales letters and catalogs to the sender.

EXTRA TIP: The OHIO (Only Handle It Once) principle helps you be more productive. It is based on the principle that everything you pick up should be done immediately. For example, every incoming invoice should be requested electronically immediately, and every magazine that lands in the mailbox should be unsubscribed immediately. This prevents time loss due to reprocessing and the accumulation of unfinished tasks.

Cell Phone / iPad

Who doesn't know their mobile phone's many photos, videos, apps, and notes? For me, it was high time to remedy this. First, I looked through my contact list and deleted all the names I couldn't remember. In addition, I removed all the people with whom I no longer had or did not want to have any contact. I did the same thing when I wasn't sure if the data was still current.

I then deleted all the apps I didn't use anymore and created a folder for the apps I rarely needed. I also checked my notes and deleted the ones I no longer needed. I unfollowed any Instagram accounts that didn't make me happy, annoyed me, or didn't generate useful content. On Facebook, I kicked out all my friends who weren't friends.

The most tedious part was sorting through the photos. To do this, I created different albums and assigned the pictures accordingly. I deleted bad and similar photos. I saved old pictures or those related to my work in a folder on Dropbox.

There are a few easy-to-use and free apps for sorting photos. Here is a selection:

Google Photos: For non-IT-savvy people like me, 'Google Photos' is a good choice. The app is easy to use and offers automatic organization of images based on data, locations, and facial recognition. This makes it easy to find and sort photos. It also has a 'Clean-up' feature, which allows you to detect and delete bad or similar photos and screenshots. The app is available for Android and iOS and can also be used on the web.

Gemini is a premium paid app that can detect similar photos and duplicates on your device. Gemini also offers a feature called Smart Select, which allows you to remove all duplicates except for the top-rated pictures automatically. In addition to the premium version, there is a free trial version that you can download and check out.

After decluttering my smartphone, I saved a lot of time because I only had the apps and contacts on the device that I really needed. My phone was clean and tidy, and the storage space was also not exhausted to the last byte.

Declutter your phone and iPad. Here's how:

1. Delete unnecessary apps
2. Sort remaining apps by frequency of use and group them into folders
3. Check and update note-taking apps, remove unnecessary and outdated notes
4. Delete unwanted photos or move them to the cloud
5. Check social media accounts and unfollow them if necessary
6. Check, update, and delete unnecessary entries
7. Go through WhatsApp chats, quit groups (I know, an awkward affair...), and archive chats.

EXTRA TIP: If you leave the first page of your phone blank and choose an inspiring wallpaper instead, the first thing you will always see is a beautiful picture that makes you happy. The second page shows you only the apps you need regularly and often. All other apps you need less frequently can be on the following pages.

Keep Life Simple

It was now February and, therefore, time to bring the previous year's documents into the archive. We kept our archive in the basement. It contained both personal and business documents. I kept an Excel sheet with all the documents in the archive to ensure a better overview. I kept archiving in general simple: I updated the Excel sheet accordingly when I brought the folder with the previous year's documents into the archive.

My life had become much easier since I now only had to worry about one business. Of course, it was also less stressful. However, our income had decreased significantly. That was what I was most afraid of, which was why I hadn't pulled the ripcord sooner. But ultimately, it was only thanks to this crisis that I was able to muster the courage to do something about my situation. Difficult times can also be guideposts that help us to reflect on what is essential and lead us back on the right path.

It made me realize again that my family was the most important thing in my life. The top priority per se. Because when I think about the past, it wasn't our possessions but the memories of the times with my children that touched me the most. And that's exactly what I wanted: to spend more time with my children again, intensively without mentally going through my business to-do list – just enjoying the moment in the here and now with my sweet boys.

I was all the more pleased that we had now started planning our six-month break in the USA. This trip had been planned for a long time, but we had to postpone it for a year due to the pandemic. Now that I had finally sorted out my business mess, it seemed like the perfect time to do it. When I was decluttering, it helped me to think that we would be abroad for a long time. Since we planned to sublet our apartment for six months, it was easier for me to get rid of unnecessary things. On the one hand, we then had to pack less stuff to store in the basement. On the other hand, I asked myself for each item whether I would take it with me if we stayed in the USA forever.

In the meantime, I replaced my precisely scheduled daily plan with a bullet journal. This personalized planning system, which combines a diary, calendar, notebook, and organizer, allowed me to organize my appointments, tasks, goals, and thoughts in one place. I liked the flexibility and adaptability to my individual needs and that I could design and adapt it to my preferences.

Accordingly, my bullet journal was not one of those elaborately designed masterpieces that are always presented to me on social media. My bullet journal only has a simple design that includes what I consider to be the most important issues for life goals, finances, and ideas. It helped me better pursue my goals and express my creativity by writing down all the thoughts floating around in my head. By putting them on paper, I freed up my mind and was able to calm down better. It also sharpened my awareness of slow living and mindfulness. During my time as a busy businesswoman, these topics had no place in my everyday life. But now that the businesswoman was gone, the doors to gratitude and leisure opened. What had previously been a burden for me and prevented me from working, I could now tackle with joy and inner peace. Whether I was standing in the kitchen cooking for my family or walking in the woods. I enjoyed it again, and it made me truly happy. At least the walks in the forest did.

I also wanted to approach the topic of 'money' in a more relaxed manner. Because we knew we would have to make do with less income in the future, we took a serious and strategic look at our finances for the first time. We sought advice from independent financial mentors who were so young they could have been our children. But we didn't see any disadvantage in this. On the contrary, we carefully selected these young people because we saw them as an opportunity not to miss out on the changes in the monetary economy – because one thing was for sure: the financial system with which we had grown up was changing, and the era of the old-established silver foxes in the banks was slowly coming to an end.

We acquired more and more financial knowledge and implemented it step by step. The first thing we did was simplify our bank account chaos. My husband and I probably had around twelve accounts: joint ones for living expenses, savings accounts for the children, company accounts, pension accounts, vested benefits accounts, and various private and savings accounts for him and me. Each of these accounts costs a lot of money each month. The hefty fees of maintaining the accounts exceeded the meager interest many times over.

Once again, we did tabula rasa and canceled almost all accounts. Ultimately, my husband still had a private account and a retirement account. I kept a private account and a vested benefits account. The latter, however, is imposed. My pension money was parked there and had to remain untouched by law. My only option was to convert it into an investment fund to counteract this waste at least a little. A sustainable, passively managed one. After all, converting it into a fund increased the chance of generating income, while the money in the account inevitably lost value due to inflation. We also closed our boys' savings accounts and opened a stock/ETF portfolio with an online broker.

At the same time, we also realized that we had to reduce our fixed costs to a minimum if we wanted to be free and flexible. That's why my husband and I looked through all our insurance policies and checked whether they were really necessary – and, if so, whether the insured amount was realistic.

We made a list of all the subscriptions and canceled any we didn't absolutely need. It had to be cut as part of our savings if it wasn't essential to our work but just a nice addition. This enabled us to reduce our monthly subscription costs from over 800 francs to a quarter of that.

We also wrote an overview of all our income and expenses. We also created a budget for our grocery shopping and other expenses. This gave us a good overview, and we saw the numbers in black and white. In practice, we noticed that if we economized, we could get along quite well with less income. Of course, our goal was still to build up passive income, but that didn't happen overnight. But we could start today so that we can lead a self-determined life in the future. A gentle, peaceful, and simple life. I think that would be enough for me.

The Children's School Supplies

Before the winter vacation, the children brought home many notebooks, drawings, and handicrafts. I took this as an opportunity to finally take care of their old school things. Of course, I needed the help of my two sons. Together, we looked through everything and decided what we wanted to keep. We sorted out old schoolbooks and notebooks, but we kept the essay books because the children had described their special experiences in them. Rereading the essays later and reminiscing about past events is always fun. We also kept some selected drawings in individual baskets for each child. The rest was allowed to leave our home.

EXTRA TIP: As an alternative to physical storage, you can photograph the drawings and crafts and create a lovely photo book.

Children's Room

During our decluttering campaign, it turned out that my children had a preference for material things. Nevertheless, it was no problem for them to part with unnecessary belongings. They were willing when I suggested cleaning out their rooms. My secondborn even turned out to be a real decluttering master. We sat together on the floor and went through his toys, from the single Lego brick to the tractors to the manure setter. He quickly and decisively decided what he wanted to keep and what he didn't. So we rushed through his possessions like Elon Musk's Falcon 9 through space.

When we went to the wardrobe, he knew exactly what he wanted to wear and what clothes he would never leave the house with. The decluttering had a remarkable positive effect: his closet now offered enough space for clothes that were still too big for him and that had previously been stored in a box in the basement. That way, I didn't have an overview of the clothes we still had and often missed the right time, so the clothes were sometimes too small for him when I brought them upstairs.

In the teen cave of the firstborn, I followed the same pattern. He, too, had no trouble deciding what he wanted to keep and what he didn't. There was only one difference: my teenager was attached to more possessions than his younger brother, which was perfectly fine. It was very important to me not to force anyone to part with things they wanted to keep. I was convinced that it wouldn't be helpful to impose my penchant for reduction on the boys. It was all the nicer to observe how happy the children were about their clean and tidy rooms.

Here is a little input on what you could sort through with the kiddies:

☐ Clothes

☐ Ski suits, hats, gloves

☐ Shoes

☐ Broken and unused toys

☐ Books

☐ Board games

☐ Handicrafts materials

☐ Crayons of all kinds

☐ Paper, Cut-Out Sheets

☐ Puzzles and individual puzzle pieces

☐ Posters and pictures

☐ Instruments

☐ Sports equipment

☐ Video games

☐ Odds and ends: fidget spinners, toys from children's candy, trading cards, stickers, key chains, etc.

EXTRA TIP: What is useful in general also applies to the children's room: each object needs its own home. When everything is in its place, the little ones know exactly where to find their things. And even better, they also know where to put things back in. So, bring on the baskets, (treasure) boxes, and drawers, sort all the Lego bricks, vehicles, books, and puzzles, and give everything a home.

For the firstborn, I also labeled the desk drawers with the names of the various school subjects. He could have packed up his school supplies in a flash in a perfect world. Of course, it didn't work for us. But what are you going to do when the teenager celebrates the chaos and prefers to spread his school stuff widely scattered on his desk ...

Storage Room or Closet

I love our storage room! It offers us enough space for cleaning utensils, tools, vases, supplies, and much more. And precisely because you store so many different things in storage rooms or closets, it quickly gets messy there.

Totally motivated, I got to work and cleared out the entire storage room. At the same time, I sorted everything according to categories, such as cleaning utensils and cleaning products, supplies, tools, etc. After that, I put away one category after the other, thus creating a clear structure.

The effect was astounding. And although we are only talking about a storage room here, the room now radiated so much tranquility that we were filled with a feeling of joy and satisfaction every time we entered. In addition, everything was now easily accessible, and we could quickly and easily find what we needed.

Organize your storage room or closet in just a few steps:

1. Clear everything out
2. Sort items by category, such as cleaning utensils, tools, supplies, medicines, etc.
3. Declutter one category at a time
4. Use shelves, storage boxes, or other storage solutions to create a clear structure when putting things away.

When everything is in place, your storage room becomes a place of joy and order rather than being synonymous with chaos. You'll be surprised how much space you can gain through this reorganization and how much easier your life will be as a result.

Medication

1. Sort medications according to application area: pain, cold, allergies, etc. Medical aids should also be clearly arranged: band-aids, bandages, etc.

2. Check the expiration date of the medicines. IMPORTANT: Take medication to the pharmacy for disposal. If it ends up in household waste, it can end up in the soil or groundwater, posing a danger to animals, plants, and the environment.

3. Don't forget vitamins and supplements, and check their expiration date, too.

EXTRA TIP: I bought the 'MOPPE' at Ikea – a small piece of furniture with drawers. Each category of medication was given a drawer, which I labeled accordingly (with the P-touch, of course). So I can find the medicine I'm looking for in no time!

Vases, Mason Jars, and Other Glass Containers

I had more than enough vases, although I only set out bouquets in spring and summer. In the end, I only kept a small and a large vase – the two I liked the most. All the others went – exactly, you guessed it – into the 'Toni box.'

EXTRA TIP: The home remedy baking soda can make heavily soiled vases clean again in no time. Simply dissolve a packet of baking soda in warm water in the vase, let it sit for some time, scrub, and you're done.

Supplies

After I had to pack boxes of groceries and drugstore items during our last move, I decided to stop stockpiling as a matter of principle. The only exception I made was for essential medicines. For everything else, if I can buy the product at any time and for less than 20 francs, I don't have to have any extras in the house. At least in theory. In practice, unfortunately, it seemed that despite my good intentions, some supplies had accumulated in the meantime, which now had to be sorted. First, I sorted the items by category: toothpaste, replacement toothbrush heads, shower gels, cleaning rags, etc. After that, I put everything away so that we could see at a glance what we still had in stock. In this way, unnecessary purchases could be avoided in the future.

These supplies can be used up and cleared out:

☐ Cleaning products and cleaning utensils such as rags and sponges

☐ Toothpaste, toothbrushes, dental floss

☐ Shower gel, shampoos, deodorants, soaps, sunscreen

☐ Light bulbs and batteries

Cleaning Products

We had so many cleaning products, rags, and sponges that I had to seriously wonder where all that stuff came from. In any case, I started by sorting everything by category: window cleaners, toilet cleaners, kitchen cleaners, car care products, etc. Then, I filled the bottles with refills and put together a cleaning basket for myself. So, I quickly had all the cleaning utensils I needed regularly. I also stowed the car cleaning and care products in a separate car cleaning box.

In the future, I decided to replace every used cleaning agent with ecological alternatives such as vinegar, baking soda, or citric acid. This will allow us to reduce our collection of cleaning products to a minimum and also help to reduce our environmental impact.

Electrical Appliances & Cables

Cables everywhere you looked. Power strips, extension cords, internet cables, and various cables to charge anything (maybe Skechers or the children's bike lights?). I didn't have a plan. It was a real cable nightmare. I first assigned the charging cables to the corresponding devices to get an overview. I wrapped the ones I could identify with duct tape and labeled them accordingly. I disposed of the unassignable cables. Of the rest of the cables, I kept only the ones we needed regularly: an extension cord and a power strip.

I also chose to dispose of a Blu-ray device, two old laptops, two flashlights, and a cell phone, making sure to do so properly. I had the laptops' hard drives erased by a professional. I was a bit paranoid since I also had sensitive client data on the old devices. I wanted to ensure that all data was permanently deleted and that it was really gone, not that it was still floating around in a hidden trash bin somewhere.

Order for electrical appliances – a little inspiration on what you can check and declutter if necessary:

☐ Defective electrical appliances: radios, CD players, mobile phones, laptops, etc.

☐ Extension cords

☐ Charging cables of any kind

☐ Internet, printer cables, etc.

☐ Power strips

☐ Flashlights

Tools

Personally, I would only need a hammer and maybe a yard-stick. My husband needs a few more tools, but certainly not everything in multiple versions. So, we sorted out the ones we had in duplicates and triplicates. In addition, we had tons of anchors and screws of all kinds that we would not have needed in a hundred years. I took the discarded things to our friend Toni, who wanted them. For the tools we wanted to keep, we got a toolbox.

EXTRA TIP: Nowadays, you don't have to own every drill bit and saw yourself. Simply ask your neighbor or rent on appropriate platforms or at the Bauhaus.

Wrapping Material for Gifts

We had an abundance of wrapping paper, ribbons, and pendants. I was also able to reduce a lot in this area. I immediately disposed of paper that was too small, crumpled, or thick, as it was unsuitable for wrapping gifts. I also looked through all the ribbons, pendants, and gift bags and sorted out everything I didn't like anymore.

For a long time, I hadn't been able to find a practical storage solution for wrapping paper and accessories. That's why I temporarily used the kickboard packaging, which is well suited for this because of its long, flat shape. Not the most elegant solution, but at least the remaining wrapping paper was neatly stored. When I was at IKEA some time ago, I finally found a suitable container. I took 'SKUBB' home with me and am very satisfied with its services so far.

EXTRA TIP: To prevent the wrapping paper from constantly unrolling and crumbling, I cut open the cardboard of a used toilet paper roll lengthwise and put it over the wrapping paper roll. This will keep the paper firmly in place and make it look neat. In this way, it can also be stored vertically in the basket.

Miscellaneous

When deciding which things I wanted to keep, I always asked myself the following questions: Do I use the item at all? And what amount is realistic? For example, we had far too many empty cardboard boxes should we need to ship something. In addition, it turned out that we had never used the iron and ironing board that my husband dragged with him into our marriage. It may be because I had no idea how an iron worked, as I had never ironed in my life. And because I didn't plan to do so in the future either, I sold the device online.

Miscellaneous items that often accumulate unnoticed:

□ Empty cardboard boxes

□ Paper bags, plastic bags, jute bags, etc.

□ Unused household appliances, such as iron and ironing board

□ Small spare parts and special tools for furniture

□ DIY materials you don't need anymore

□ Key chains

□ Keys that no one knows what they're for anymore

□ Cable ties, tape

□ Batteries

□ Ashtrays

External Reduction = Inner Peace

I was happy. I hadn't felt as relaxed and content in months. I was indescribably grateful that I could finally dedicate myself entirely to my children without constantly having a never-ending to-do list in the back of my mind. I enjoyed my daily walks through the forest, where I could switch off wonderfully. I could have continued walking for hours, especially in cloudy, rainy weather. I also treated myself to regular visits to the beautician for permanent hair removal. This was another step towards making my life easier. By the way, I was also able to dispose of shaving cream and plastic razors. And after each of these appointments, I couldn't wait to rush to Starbucks to get my beloved latte.

I have only worked through to-do lists and managed everyday tasks in the past few years. I had completely forgotten how soothing it felt to do something just for me. Of course, I enjoyed working. I loved challenges, and there were times when I really thrived the more work I had. But my life didn't stop. The circumstances around me changed. The children grew older, had different needs, and needed more support in school matters. I also got older, and my focus shifted – away from career and material things towards the desire for a more leisurely pace of life. The balance between work and free time has been out of balance for me for a long time. The balance was out of control because I only got up in the morning to work on to-dos. A few years ago, I was able to cope with this easily. But now I felt increasingly rushed, empty, and burned out. I was really annoyed, and words can hardly describe how tired I was of all the business bullshit! And no amount of money in the world could have compensated for that in any way. Because if it costs my inner peace, it's definitely too expensive. Interestingly, my act of liberation, let's call it, began with decluttering my material environment, but it ended with a feeling of inner peace. I created space for new energy with every item I removed from my home and every business relationship that left my mind. It seemed as if external reduction and inner peace went hand in hand.

Even though it was spring, the temperatures were already summery. I thought it was a good time to tackle the basement as it was also a welcome opportunity to escape the unbearable sun. For me, hardly anything reduced my mood and motivation to zero more quickly than a bright sun shining from the sky. Summer and I would never be friends. I would have loved to do it like Princess Vlad: Waiting upside down somewhere in the dark until it was finally September again. Everyone who ever met me found this so otherworldly that in the past, I had felt compelled to ask my parents if we had Transylvanian ancestors. But every time, my father answered the same thing: He didn't know because I fell off the shelf into their shopping cart at the grocery store. This answer actually explains a lot. Anyway, I grabbed my husband and explained my plan to him. He had to help because some of his things were stored in the basement. I would never throw away family members' items without asking.

Basement / Attic / Garage

First, we emptied the entire basement. After that, my husband sorted out his personal belongings and documents, and I devoted myself to our archive. First, I sorted all the documents by year and whether they were personal or business in nature. Then, I packed them into boxes, sorted them by year, and labeled them with contents and year. Since I had to fall back on old documents from time to time, it was important to me that I could find them quickly in the future.

In the end, we decided together what to do with the stored things that belonged to both of us. Finally, we gave away two out of three sleeping bags. We also parted with a tent, various shoes, outdoor toys, and old suitcases. Two sleds and two fans, which we had never needed, were also allowed to go.

We couldn't believe we now had a half-empty basement! Everything that was left in it had its raison d'être. We were done with the times when everything was put in the basement just so it was quickly out of the way and we didn't have to worry about the actual benefit. Because in my mind and my subconscious, all the stuff was still there.

With a big grin on our faces, we waved after Toni's van, which once again drove away full to the brim with our stuff.

You could clear out the following items in the basement, attic, or garage:

□ Sports equipment and articles

□ Sleds, skis, and snowboards

□ Camping equipment

□ Outdoor articles

□ Hobby utensils and toys

□ Summer and winter shoes

□ Shoe polish kit

□ Children's clothes and shoes that are too small

□ Old furniture and fixtures that you don't like or need anymore

□ Boxes, cans, bottles, clothes, etc. for the recycling center

□ Leftover paint and other building materials that you no longer need

□ Pest control products

□ Automotive accessories and equipment, as well as old tires

My Simple Joys

There were still four weeks until we left for America. We were well on schedule with most of the preparations. The photos of our apartment for the rental platform were in the can, and we also found a 'babysitter' for our Tesla. Most of our belongings were already packed, and redirecting our (now sparse) mail to my sister was also underway. All the necessary documents and letters for the embassy were ready. The only thing that we were running short on time was our visa. Although we had already submitted the visa application in February, we didn't get our appointment at the embassy until the beginning of July, two weeks before our departure. Since we couldn't change the circumstances and I had vowed to stop worrying in advance, we took it as it came. We also had countless other appointments: a surgery date for our secondborn, dental and doctor appointments for almost the entire family, school plays, birthday dinners, and a meeting with the online school that took over the lessons for our boys while we were in America.

To my delight, my husband had now also realized how liberating decluttering can be. Since we only took two large suitcases and two pieces of hand luggage for our entire family, we were only able to take the bare minimum with us anyway. That's why he decided to go through the rest of his things and free himself from baggage.

For once, my Amazon business didn't cause any problems. At least none that required quick intervention. My products were bought, but the advertising costs were so high that I had to look for the profit with a magnifying glass. I was aware of this problem and had already instructed my account manager to change the advertising campaigns. And then, out of the blue, I received good news from my shipping company: My goods, which were on the damaged ship, had already arrived in perfect condition at my interim storage facility in North Carolina. What a wonderful feeling when problems solve themselves! I was thrilled by this great news and felt confirmed by my realization that it was not worth worrying about things that have not yet arrived or whose outcome is uncertain.

Between the many appointments during our travel preparations, I sometimes wondered how I would have managed it all if I hadn't drastically reduced my professional commitments. Gradually, I realized that I had been just functioning for years. I had to use all my energy to get through the day. Now, I could finally enjoy the little joys of everyday life again. I wouldn't have thought it possible that a hyacinth's sweet, floral scent could delight me so much. The pleasant atmosphere of a clear summer morning filled me with contentment, and the fresh smell of hay in the evening hours took me back to my carefree youth when I spent every day with my cousin at the horse farm. I was eternally grateful for my family and everything I owned. The further my husband and I moved away from our over-filled lives, the more we discovered the potential and possibilities of our new life. And that was a priceless benefit for our entire family.

Letting go of things that no longer served us was a significant step toward a simpler and more fulfilling life. Skipping news and weather forecasts has also proven to be effective. We realized that consuming news wasn't doing us any good. That wasn't surprising because 99% of the reports were negative and mostly didn't even affect us directly. Nevertheless, they negatively impacted our psyche and were also bad for a positive outlook on life. That's why one evening, we decided to stop watching this flood of negative information. If something were to happen that we needed to know, we would find out anyway. So, I immediately deleted all news apps from my smartphone.

From this point on, we also skipped the weather forecast. For years, I had been annoyed by the judgmental presentation: the sun and high temperatures were portrayed as good, while the prospect of rain and clouds put on terribly sad faces. But do they really want it never to rain and the sun to shine every day? So, get rid of the weather forecasts. From then on, I took the weather as it came, and my husband was happy that he no longer had to endure my sarcastic co-hosting of the forecasts. I relegated the weather app to the back folder of my phone, which I rarely opened. I would have preferred to delete it completely, but I didn't want to miss out on the severe weather warnings. Not yet.

We feel more peaceful and carefree since we skip the news and weather reports. It was a good decision, and it became increasingly clear that we were on the right path.

EXTRA TIP: If you don't want to rely solely on the grapevine to stay informed, there are various ways to receive personalized messages. For example, many Internet browsers allow you to customize your homepage to show you your favorite news sources. Numerous news apps also tailor the content displayed to your interests, reading behavior, and activities.

Final Stretch

Our apartment looked almost like an Airbnb – and it should because we would be on our plane to Miami in two weeks' time. Yes, I know, Miami: endless summer, sun, and unbearably hot. It's definitely not my dream destination. But it was a great starting point for our East Coast trip. It was also once again a great opportunity to overcome my misgivings and get involved in something I normally wouldn't have been prepared to do. I couldn't wait until the adventure started. This trip was important for our family, so my restless husband finally had to slow down, but also so that the boys could be far away from their game consoles. It was also important for me, so I had to get out of my cozy comfort zone. I felt like this was urgently needed to avoid becoming even weirder than I already was. Nowadays, I even feel uncomfortable when I go to the mailbox and there is no mail in it because I don't want to be seen if I have to sneak back into the house without having done anything. It sounds insane when I write about it. My firstborn would grimace whenever I asked him to check the mailbox after school. Shaking his head and smiling, he did it politely, only to comment on it with, "You're so lost!" Furthermore, I couldn't imagine what it would be like to not have a permanent home for so long and to have to find my way in new places constantly. I didn't know how I would cope with never being able to be alone for six months. I really liked being alone so I could indulge in my ideas and feed my thoughts. But I felt I was ready to get involved in these experiences. Luckily, nothing stood in our way now because our appointment at the American embassy in Bern went smoothly, and we received the visa. We then took advantage of the opportunity to take a stroll through the capital and imagine what it would be like if we took such trips to American cities. But until then, the boys went to school as usual for the last few days before we left – and I still had time to worry about photos and photo albums.

Photos and Photo Albums

We had about twenty albums, a box of loose pictures, and five photo books. First, I looked through all the loose photos and eliminated the boring, blurry, and similar ones. I also sorted out pictures that made me sad or evoked negative feelings. I only kept a few souvenir photos per event.

I did the same with the albums. I took out all the pictures I wanted to keep and threw away the rest. I admit it wasn't easy (guilty conscience, bad karma...). But let's be honest: When would I ever look at four photo albums from my wedding again? In addition, there were so many double, triple, and sometimes even quadruple images that you almost had to force yourself to plow through all four albums. And that couldn't be the goal. We only looked at our photo books regularly. They were placed in our living room for easy access and looked much more inviting than the heavy, old-fashioned albums.

To make the decision easier for me, I asked myself with every photo: Does it make me happy? Does it give me fond memories? Is it a picture worthy of a photo book? If the answer was 'yes' three times, I scanned it. Afterward, I created beautiful photo books on various topics, such as Holidays in New York 2017.

I had already sorted and deleted my surplus cell phone photos. I also wanted to use the rest I had saved in my Dropbox to create photo books. However, this project turned out to be very time-consuming, so I didn't have time for it before we left. It's on my list for next year.

Here's how to get your photo collection organized:

1. Gather all the pictures (the loose ones and the albums).

2. Sort out the images that you don't want to keep because they don't bring you joy, make you sad, are of poor quality, or are duplicates.

3. Scan loose photos to store them digitally and save space.

4. Create inviting photo books that you can enjoy.

EXTRA TIP: There are fantastic free smartphone apps to scan analog photos. For instance:

1. **Google Fotoscan:** This app is easy to use and achieves good quality when scanning photos. It removes reflections and provides automatic alignment to make scanning easier.

2. **CamScanner:** This app is also very easy to use and offers high image quality.

Scanning photos can be extremely time-consuming. If you have a lot of analog images, you might want to consider outsourcing the scan job to an appropriate service provider.

Garden, Terrace, Balcony

Two days before we left, I took care of our garden. This consisted only of a small lawn surrounded by bushes. For this reason, and also because neither of us was fond of gardening, we hardly had any gardening tools or other equipment. Nevertheless, I found a few items that we could dispose of: two charred garden chairs (the secondborn wanted to convert them into an outdoor stove), a small rusted stove, a fire bowl, and a flower pot. Additionally, we sold our gas grill, as it had been unused for the past three years. We used the mini oven for grilling, which was now unfortunately rusted.

Tidying up outdoors – a small recommendation on what you could declutter outside:

□ Gardening supplies and tools

□ Defective garden furniture

□ BBQ, fire bowls

□ Garden hose and attachments

□ Damaged fences

□ Old, broken flowerpots and boxes

□ Outdated and defective garden lighting or solar lights

□ Worn gardening gloves or workwear

□ Outdated or broken garden décor

□ Dead plants

The Joy of Letting Go

Now it was finally here, the day of our departure! We have been looking forward to this day for two years. And yet, I had the feeling that it was only yesterday when we were looking for a suitable Airbnb somewhere in the Northeast of the USA on our laptop. Basically, all four of us were extremely modest – or so my husband and I thought, but Generation Z and Alpha would teach us otherwise in the USA. In any case, our modesty did not necessarily mean that not everyone had their own little individual needs that needed to be considered when looking for suitable accommodation. So, the teenager absolutely had to have a hospital within acceptable proximity to the house. All toilet bowls had to be white for the secondborn, and my husband wanted a Tesla Supercharger not far from our home. And as far as I was concerned, I definitely couldn't do without a fireplace, but I could do without neighbors.

Eventually, we settled on a beautiful white wooden house with an impressive red brick chimney rising up the side of the house. A white picket fence surrounded the semicircular entrance and exit, and a swing dangled from a massive oak tree next to the entrance. Dark gray wooden shutters flanked the cute lattice windows, and at the front, there was an inviting bay window with large picture windows. I already imagined my husband and I sitting on the small porch, drinking coffee, and the boys running around the large, wooded property. The house, built in the typical colonial style, was located in the Hudson Valley, approximately 150 kilometers north of New York City.

But before we could embark on the adventure, we had to bring our personal belongings into the basement. When my husband carried the last box downstairs, we were both pleased and surprised because we even had room left. After a final check of all the rooms, I closed the front door and paused for a moment. Now, the adventure actually began!

As we drove down our street in the Uber, I saw the house getting smaller and smaller in the rearview mirror. I couldn't help thinking about all our belongings, which had also left our home in the last few months. How often had I waved after Toni and his delivery truck as he drove away with a load of our discarded things? It was sobering to realize how many things we had that we neither liked nor needed and were even useless. Strangely enough, I enjoyed getting rid of them more than owning them.

Almost two years had passed since I decided on that October morning, exhausted and refuted, that something had to change – that I had to change to eliminate the oppressive state of being overwhelmed. And when I hesitantly began decluttering the first things, I never would have dreamed that this inconspicuous act would result in so many drastic changes. My husband and I not only let go of hundreds of items but also a house, two Teslas, two companies, an office, and one or two unpleasant people. We have never regretted these decisions.

Possessions can be stressful. Now, we feel lighter, freer, and more grateful for everything we still have. We no longer waste time managing, caring for, moving around, or maintaining unnecessary items. Instead, we develop an awareness of what is really important in our lives. We rarely make impulse purchases anymore because, before each purchase, we think about whether we really need the product and whether it would give us as much joy as the things we already own.

What will happen next after our stay in America? I will certainly make our household more sustainable and integrate more mindfulness into my life. I also want to give my four top priorities the time they deserve: First and foremost are my family in general and my children in particular. I also want to finally write my novel, optimize my finances, and get more exercise. I would also like to simplify other areas of my life. So, this journey is far from over!

How will my business continue? I have no idea. I want to let life come to me. What will go can go. What will come may come. Or maybe not. I don't always have to have a plan. Only one thing is certain: I would still rather live in a barn with an outhouse than ever again feel as terribly unhappy and drained as I did on that foggy October morning.

A Good Idea

✓ Approach decluttering with joy and enjoy the ease of letting go.

✓ Be honest with yourself.

✓ Courageously face the unpleasant decisions.

✓ Take your time.

✓ Reserve a box for the items that you can't part with yet, for whatever reason.

✓ Look at the box again in a year and make a new decision.

✓ When in doubt, it's better to keep a little too much than to give things away too early.

✓ Keep as many things as you need to feel comfortable and happy. If your large collection of books makes you immensely happy – fantastic, keep it.

✓ Think about the atmosphere you want in your home and then say 'no' to everything that doesn't match it.

Not a Good Idea

✗ Disposing of your partner's or children's belongings without asking.

✗ Not getting discarded items out of the house fast enough.

✗ Spending too much time selling items. The effort of photographing, describing, answering questions, and packaging is often not worth it.

✗ Setting a numerical limit for items that you are 'allowed' to own. Unlike Amazon, decluttering is NOT a numbers game.

✗ Listen to what others say. Each individual's possessions and needs are unique. That's why everyone decides on their own how many possessions they want to have in their lives and what can go.

✗ Stressing and not trusting the process. Decluttering is a journey that can take years. Therefore, it is important to remain patient and create an environment where you feel comfortable in the long term.

Last But Not Least

I wrote this book during our six-month trip to the US East Coast. Strictly speaking, in the idyllic town of Rhinebeck in New York State. On the edge of the Hudson River, surrounded by the colorful forests of the Hudson Valley, the charming homes, and loving residents, it was truly easy to be inspired. I was actually looking forward to finishing my novel. But when I was almost overwhelmed by countless decorative pieces and furniture in our pretty house with the big fireplace, the white toilets, and not far from the hospital and the Tesla Supercharger, I was overcome by an irrepressible desire to declutter. Because I obviously couldn't clear out Theresa's Airbnb, I started writing about my search for a simpler life instead. The words flowed effortlessly onto the screen, and for the first time in years, I got into a flow that felt light and buoyant. After the last line was written and the legendary Indian summer stood outside in its perfect beauty, I was overcome by that pleasant warmth of freedom and contentment that I had longed for so much over the last few years.